CONTENTS

GREEN BEAN CASSEROLE

MAKES 5 SERVINGS | PREP: 10 minutes **BAKE:** 30 minutes

- 1 can (10½ ounces) **Campbell's**® Condensed Cream of Mushroom Soup (Regular **or** 98% Fat Free)
- ½ cup milk
- 1 teaspoon soy sauce
- Dash ground black pepper
- 2 packages (10 ounces **each**) frozen cut green beans, cooked and drained
- 1 can (2.8 ounces) French fried onions (1⅓ cups)

1 Stir the soup, milk, soy sauce, black pepper, green beans and **⅔ cup** onions in a 1½-quart casserole.

2 Bake at 350°F. for 25 minutes or until hot. Stir the green bean mixture.

3 Sprinkle the remaining onions over the green bean mixture. Bake for 5 minutes more or until onions are golden brown.

KITCHEN TIP

You can also make this classic side dish with fresh or canned green beans. You will need either 1½ pounds fresh green beans, cut into 1-inch pieces, cooked and drained, **or 2 cans** (about 16 ounces **each**) cut green beans, drained, for the frozen green beans.

BEEF TACO BAKE

MAKES 4 SERVINGS | PREP: 10 minutes **BAKE:** 30 minutes

- 1 pound ground beef
- 1 can (10¾ ounces) **Campbell's**® Condensed Tomato Soup
- 1 cup **Pace**® Picante Sauce
- ½ cup milk
- 6 flour tortillas (8-inch) **or** corn tortillas (6-inch), cut into 1-inch pieces
- 1 cup shredded Cheddar cheese (about 4 ounces)

1 Cook the beef in a 10-inch skillet over medium-high heat until well browned, stirring often. Pour off any fat.

2 Stir the soup, picante sauce, milk, tortillas and **half** the cheese in the skillet. Spoon the beef mixture into a 2-quart shallow baking dish. Cover the baking dish.

3 Bake at 400°F. for 30 minutes or until the beef mixture is hot and bubbling. Sprinkle with the remaining cheese.

TASTY 2-STEP CHICKEN

MAKES 4 SERVINGS | PREP: 5 minutes **COOK:** 20 minutes

- 1 tablespoon vegetable oil
- 4 skinless, boneless chicken breast halves (about 1 pound)
- 1 can (10½ ounces) **Campbell's**® Condensed Cream of Mushroom Soup (Regular, 98% Fat Free **or Healthy Request**®)
- ½ cup water

1 Heat the oil in a 10-inch skillet over medium-high heat. Add the chicken and cook for 10 minutes or until well browned on both sides. Remove the chicken from the skillet.

2 Stir the soup and water in the skillet and heat to a boil. Return the chicken to the skillet. Reduce the heat to low. Cover and cook for 5 minutes or until the chicken is cooked through.

KITCHEN TIP

This recipe is also delicious with **Campbell's**® Condensed Cream of Mushroom with Roasted Garlic Soup **or** Cream of Chicken with Herbs Soup.

SLOW COOKER SIMPLE BEEF BOURGUIGNONNE

MAKES 6 SERVINGS | PREP: 10 minutes **COOK:** 8 hours

- 1 can (10¾ ounces) **Campbell's**® Condensed Golden Mushroom Soup
- 1 cup Burgundy **or** other dry red wine
- 2 cloves garlic, minced
- 1 teaspoon dried thyme leaves, crushed
- 2 cups small button mushrooms (about 6 ounces)
- 2 cups fresh **or** thawed frozen baby carrots
- 1 cup frozen small whole onions, thawed
- 1½ pounds beef top round steak, 1½-inches thick, cut into 1-inch pieces

1 Stir the soup, wine, garlic, thyme, mushrooms, carrots, onions and beef in a 3½-quart slow cooker.

2 Cover and cook on LOW for 8 to 9 hours* or until the beef is fork-tender.

Or on HIGH for 4 to 5 hours.

CHICKEN TETRAZZINI

MAKES 4 SERVINGS | PREP: 20 minutes **COOK:** 5 minutes

- 1 can (10½ ounces) **Campbell's**® Condensed Cream of Mushroom Soup (Regular **or** 98% Fat Free)
- ¾ cup water
- ½ cup grated Parmesan cheese
- 2 tablespoons chopped fresh parsley **or** 2 teaspoons dried parsley flakes
- ¼ cup chopped red pepper **or** pimientos (optional)
- ½ package (8 ounces) spaghetti, cooked and drained
- 2 cans (4.5 ounces **each**) **Swanson**® Premium White Chunk Chicken Breast in Water, drained

Heat the soup, water, cheese, parsley, red pepper, if desired, spaghetti and chicken in a 2-quart saucepan over medium heat until the mixture is hot and bubbling.

BROCCOLI RICE CASSEROLE

MAKES 12 SERVINGS | PREP: 20 minutes **BAKE:** 30 minutes

½ cup (1 stick) butter

1 large onion, chopped (about 1 cup)

1 package (16 ounces) frozen chopped broccoli

⅓ cup milk

1 can (10½ ounces) **Campbell's**® Cream of Chicken Soup (Regular **or** 98% Fat Free)

1 jar (8 ounces) pasteurized process cheese sauce

1½ cups cooked regular long-grain white rice

1 Heat the butter in a 10-inch skillet over medium heat. Add the onion and cook until tender-crisp, stirring occasionally.

2 Stir the broccoli in the skillet and cook until it's tender-crisp, stirring occasionally. Stir in the milk, soup, cheese sauce and rice. Cook and stir until the cheese is melted. Pour the broccoli mixture into a 2-quart shallow baking dish.

3 Bake at 350°F. for 30 minutes or until the mixture is hot and bubbling.

JILL'S HASH BROWN CASSEROLE

MAKES 8 SERVINGS | PREP: 15 minutes **BAKE:** 45 minutes

- 1 can (10½ ounces) **Campbell's**® Condensed Cream of Mushroom Soup (Regular **or** 98% Fat Free)
- 1 container (8 ounces) sour cream
- ½ cup butter, melted (1 stick)
- 1 bag (32 ounces) frozen hash brown potatoes (about 7½ cups)
- 1 medium onion, chopped (about ½ cup)
- 1 package (8 ounces) shredded Cheddar cheese (2 cups)
- Ground black pepper
- ½ cup crushed corn flakes

1 Stir the soup, sour cream, butter, potatoes, onion and cheese in a 3-quart shallow baking dish. Season with the black pepper. Sprinkle the potato mixture evenly with the crushed corn flakes.

2 Bake at 350°F. for 45 minutes or until hot and bubbling.

CHICKEN BROCCOLI DIVAN

MAKES 4 SERVINGS | PREP: 10 minutes **BAKE:** 20 minutes

4 cups cooked broccoli florets

2 cups cubed cooked chicken

1 can (10½ ounces) **Campbell's®** Condensed Cream of Chicken Soup (Regular, 98% Fat Free **or Healthy Request®**)

⅓ cup milk

½ cup shredded Cheddar cheese (about 2 ounces)

2 tablespoons dry bread crumbs

1 tablespoon butter, melted

1 Place the broccoli and chicken into a 9-inch pie plate.

2 Stir the soup and milk in a small bowl. Pour the soup mixture over the broccoli and chicken. Sprinkle with the cheese. Stir the bread crumbs and butter in a small bowl. Sprinkle the bread crumb mixture over the cheese.

3 Bake at 450°F. for 20 minutes or until the chicken mixture is hot and bubbling.

KITCHEN TIP

For cornflake topping, substitute cornflakes for the bread crumbs and omit the butter.

EASY SUBSTITUTIONS

Substitute leftover cooked turkey, **3 cans** (4.5 ounces **each**) **or 1 can** (12.5 ounces) **Swanson®** Premium White Chunk Chicken Breast in Water, drained, for the cooked chicken.

Substitute **Campbell's®** Condensed Broccoli Cheese Soup (Regular **or** 98% Fat Free) for the Cream of Chicken Soup.

TUNA NOODLE CASSEROLE

MAKES 8 SERVINGS | PREP: 10 minutes **BAKE:** 35 minutes

2 cans (10½ ounces **each**) *Campbell's*® Condensed Cream of Mushroom Soup (Regular **or** 98% Fat Free)

1 cup milk

2 cups frozen peas

2 cans (about 10 ounces **each**) tuna, drained

½ of a 12-ounce package medium egg noodles (about 4 cups), cooked and drained

2 tablespoons dry bread crumbs

1 tablespoon butter, melted

1 Stir the soup, milk, peas, tuna and noodles in a 3-quart casserole.

2 Bake at 400°F. for 30 minutes or until the tuna mixture is hot and bubbling. Stir the tuna mixture.

3 Stir the bread crumbs and butter in a small bowl. Sprinkle the bread crumb mixture over the tuna mixture. Bake for 5 minutes or until the topping is golden brown.

SAVORY POT ROAST

MAKES 8 SERVINGS
PREP: 15 minutes **COOK:** 2 hours 50 minutes

2 tablespoons vegetable oil

1 boneless beef bottom round roast **or** chuck pot roast (3½ to 4 pounds)

1 can (10½ ounces) **Campbell's**® Condensed Cream of Mushroom Soup (Regular **or** 98% Fat Free)

1¼ cups water

1 envelope (about 1 ounce) dry onion soup and recipe mix

6 medium potatoes, cut into quarters

6 medium carrots, cut into 2-inch pieces (about 3 cups)

2 tablespoons all-purpose flour

1 Heat the oil in a 6-quart saucepot over medium-high heat. Add the beef and cook until well browned on all sides. Pour off any fat.

2 Stir the mushroom soup, **1 cup** water and soup mix in a medium bowl. Add the soup mixture to the saucepot and heat to a boil. Reduce the heat to low. Cover and cook for 1 hour 30 minutes.

3 Add the potatoes and carrots to the saucepot. Cover and cook for 1 hour or until the beef is fork-tender and the vegetables are tender. Remove the beef and vegetables to a serving platter.

4 Stir the flour and remaining water in a small bowl until the mixture is smooth. Stir the flour mixture in the saucepot. Cook and stir until the mixture boils and thickens. Serve the gravy with the beef and vegetables.

BEST-EVER MEATLOAF

MAKES 8 SERVINGS
PREP: 10 minutes **BAKE:** 1 hour 15 minutes **COOK:** 5 minutes

- 1 can (10½ ounces) *Campbell's*® Condensed Cream of Mushroom Soup (Regular **or** 98% Fat Free)
- 1 small onion, finely chopped (about ¼ cup)
- 1 egg, beaten
- 2 pounds ground beef
- ½ cup dry bread crumbs
- ½ cup water

1 Thoroughly mix ½ **cup** soup, onion, egg, beef and bread crumbs in a large bowl. Place the mixture into a 13×9×2-inch baking pan and firmly shape into an 8×4-inch loaf.

2 Bake at 350°F. for 1 hour, 15 minutes or until the meatloaf is cooked through. Let the meatloaf stand for 10 minutes before slicing.

3 Heat **2 tablespoons** pan drippings, remaining soup and water in a 1-quart saucepan over medium heat until the mixture is hot and bubbling. Serve the sauce with the meatloaf.

MEATLOAF WELLINGTON

Prepare as above but bake loaf only 1 hour. Spoon off fat. Separate **1 package** (8 ounces) refrigerated crescent rolls. Place triangles crosswise over top and down sides of meatloaf, overlapping slightly. Bake 15 minutes more until golden.

FROSTED MEATLOAF

Prepare as above but bake loaf only 1 hour. Spoon off fat. Spread **3 cups** hot, seasoned mashed potatoes over loaf; sprinkle with ½ **cup** shredded Cheddar cheese. Bake 15 to 30 minutes more until meat is done.

BEEFY TACO JOES

MAKES 8 SERVINGS | PREP: 5 minutes **COOK:** 15 minutes

- 1 pound ground beef
- 1 can (10¾ ounces) **Campbell's**® Condensed Tomato Soup
- 1 cup **Pace**® Picante Sauce
- 8 **Pepperidge Farm**® Classic Sandwich Buns with Sesame Seeds, split
- ½ cup shredded Cheddar cheese (about 2 ounces)

1 Cook the beef in a 10-inch skillet over medium-high heat until well browned, stirring often to separate the meat. Pour off any fat.

2 Stir the soup and picante sauce in the skillet and cook until the mixture is hot and bubbling. Spoon the beef mixture on the buns. Top with the cheese.

BAKED MACARONI AND CHEESE

MAKES 4 SERVINGS | PREP: 20 minutes **BAKE:** 20 minutes

- 1 can (10¾ ounces) **Campbell's**® Condensed Cheddar Cheese Soup
- ⅔ cup milk
- ⅛ teaspoon ground black pepper
- 1½ cups rotini (spiral) pasta **or** medium shell pasta (about ⅓ of a 1 pound package), cooked and drained
- 2 tablespoons plain dry bread crumbs
- 2 teaspoons butter, melted

1 Heat the oven to 400°F.

2 Stir the soup, milk, black pepper and rotini in a 1-quart casserole.

3 Stir the bread crumbs and butter in a small bowl. Sprinkle the bread crumb mixture over the rotini mixture.

4 Bake for 20 minutes or until the rotini mixture is hot and bubbling.

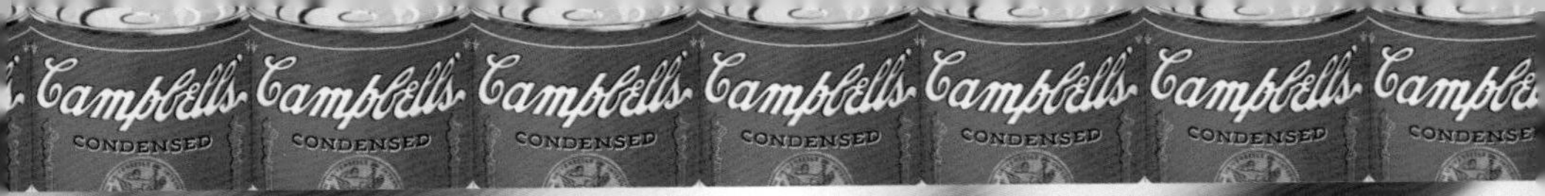
Campbell's
CONDENSED

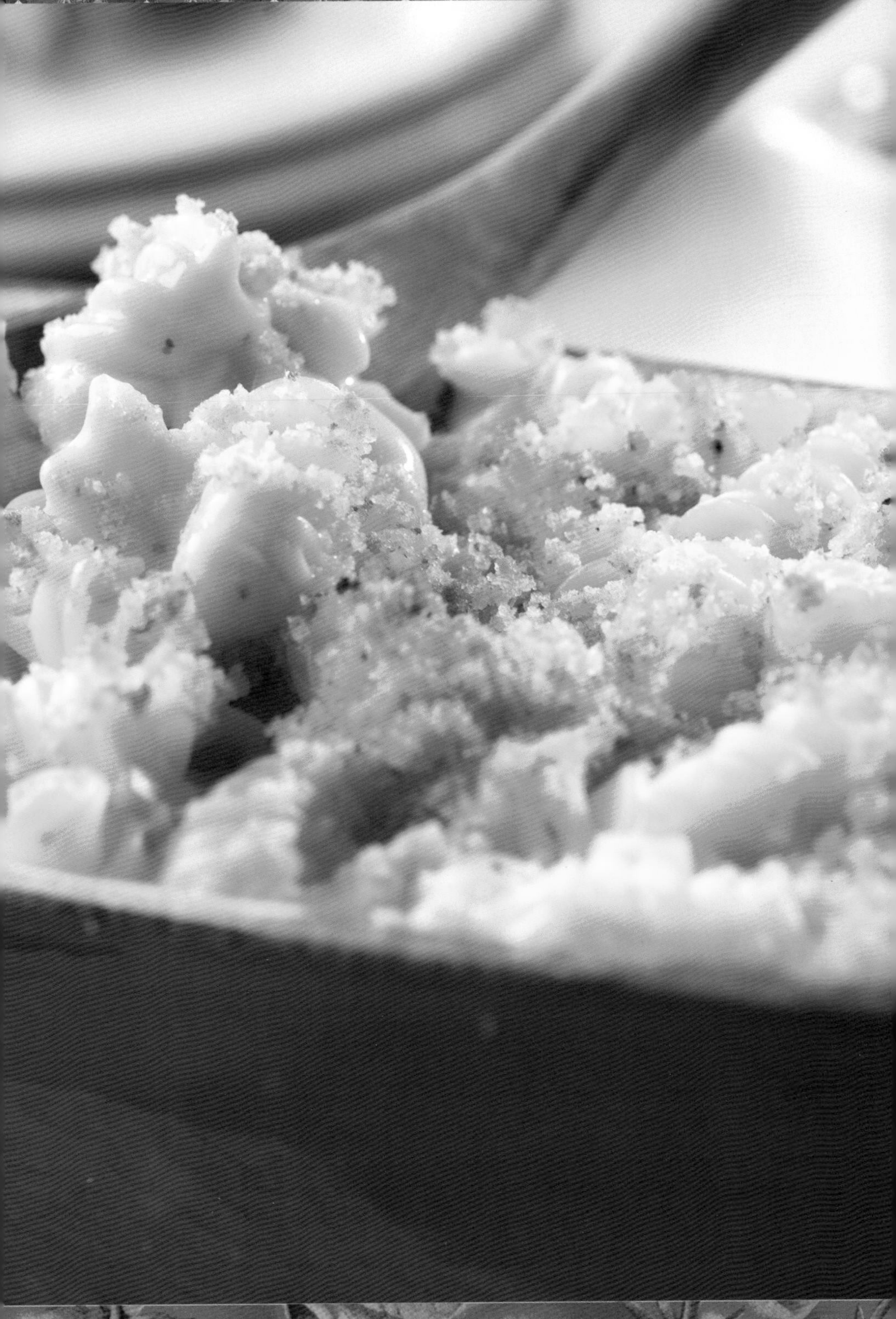

TASTY 2-STEP PORK CHOPS

MAKES 4 SERVINGS | PREP: 5 minutes **COOK:** 20 minutes

1 tablespoon vegetable oil

4 bone-in pork chops, ½-inch thick (about 1½ pounds)

1 can (10½ ounces) **Campbell's®** Condensed Cream of Mushroom Soup (Regular **or** 98% Fat Free)

½ cup water

1 Heat the oil in a 10-inch skillet over medium-high heat. Add the pork and cook until well browned on both sides.

2 Stir the soup and water in the skillet and heat to a boil. Reduce the heat to low. Cover and cook for 10 minutes or until the pork is cooked through.

KITCHEN TIP

Also great with **Campbell's®** Condensed Cream of Mushroom with Roasted Garlic Soup, with **½ cup** milk instead of water.

GARLIC PORK CHOPS

Add **1** clove garlic, minced, to the skillet with the pork chops.